Tales from an
Oxford Bench

Allan Gaw

Allan Gaw

First published 2016 by SA Press

sapress42@gmail.com

Printed by CreateSpace

British Library Cataloguing in Publication Data

A catalogue record for this book is available from the British Library

ISBN 978-0-9563242-7-6

Dedication

For Stephen, who made it all possible, and
SJ, whose smile always made the sun shine in Oxford, even in the
rain.

Allan Gaw

Contents

Acknowledgements

I need to thank all the people I met in Oxford while this book was being written—some lived there, but many, like me, were visitors. Some served me coffee, some drove taxis painted with the periodic table (where else, but Oxford) and some let me watch them and listen to them.

I would like to thank Alexandra Gaw who read the drafts of this book and took great pains not to hurt my feelings with her comments. Her gentle advice has been incorporated into the final text and I think the book is the better for it. If any clumsy writing remains, it is of course my fault and not hers.

I would also like to thank Moira Mungall at SA Press for always being an inspiration and an honest critic in equal measure.

All photographs were taken by the author.

Introduction

By Way of an Explanation

My first trip to Oxford was courtesy of Charles Ryder and Lord Sebastian Flyte, and of course Aloysius, the naughty teddy bear that needed to be spanked by an ivory-backed hair brush. Or, more correctly, by Jeremy Irons and Anthony Andrews in the shimmeringly beautiful Oxford of television's *Brideshead Revisited* — Evelyn Waugh's tale of between-the-wars love and loyalty. Watching this, I imagined that all Universities were made of honey-coloured stone and bathed in spring sunshine; that clever, good-looking people discussed great things on the lawn wearing linen suits; and I imagined that gilly flowers would bloom below my window on the quad too.

My own university experiences at Medical School in Glasgow could really not have been farther from this idyll and it would be many years before I finally visited Oxford for myself, first, as a lecturer, then as an infrequent tourist, and more recently as a regular visitor fulfilling my paternal duties because my son was studying as a postgraduate at Balliol. In all these visits I have never really lost the sense of calm I first found when walking through the streets of Oxford. There is bustle, crowds, even treacherous traffic with bikes and buses vying for the kill, but there are also stones, and trees and a rich history of scholarship quite unequalled anywhere else.

I was glad, however, that I first visited in my maturity rather than as an expectant and wide-eyed youth. I suspect Oxford can be a cruel place to those who have not yet learned that elitism is just another word for snobbery and that both can make easy victims of their prey. I suspect Oxford has broken young people — well, sadly, I know it has — but when your skin is a little thicker, you can take it at face value, and enjoy the ride without feeling you always have to justify your seat in the first class carriage.

I never studied at Oxford — I think I wish I had — but I don't know. What I do know is that I want it to be part of my life now. Its streets, its colleges and its museums all succeed without trying — effortless and beguiling. And, inspiring. Whenever I find myself in Oxford I retrace familiar steps and try to discover new paths, but what I always find is the inspiration to write. Words flow more easily by the Isis, and ideas intersect like the wakes of passing punts — gentle and unruffled.

The series of scenes presented here were written over a couple of years, sometimes in sun, sometimes in rain, but most of them on a bench in Broad Street outside Trinity and across the road from Oxfam. It's a favourite spot, not always available because I expect it's a favourite of others too, but I have come to think of it as mine as you will see in the first of the chapters. Students sometimes hurry by, and sometimes they amble. At end of term they haul large cases on uncooperative wheels over kerb stones as they move out; and at the start of a new year they carry plastic bags from Blackwell's a few doors down filled with the new knowledge they plan to acquire. A walking tour starts from here and as I sit I can watch business being drummed up and hear tourists begin by telling where home is for them. There are Americans and French,

Australians and Spanish, Koreans and, well, just about every other nationality you could mention. Broad is this street in more than name.

I sit close to the Bodleian, the Sheldonian, and the White Horse Inn, only one of which I should add serves pies, and all of Oxford seems to be within reach. The chapters that follow are as much reflections as anything else. They all take their starting point from some observation or Oxford experience, but often end up somewhere else entirely. If Oxford is about anything it is about thought. And this jumble of streets and colleges and people always makes me think. And any visitor, either in reality, or through the pages of this book, should come prepared to join the game.

What this book is not, is any kind of formal guide book. There are lots of those already and any will provide the visitor with the requisite background and maps to be able to spend a lovely day or two in Oxford. Instead, this book is about what Oxford does to your soul; how it gets under the skin and lingers long enough to change you. It has been doing this for centuries to its students, but it also makes a fair attempt with its casual visitors too. It is hard to leave Oxford unscathed and unaffected by what you will see and feel there. It is a special place as well as being completely absurd; it is absurdly beautiful as well as being absurdly traditional; it is ancient and long dead as well as being as alive as its thousands of young students.

The tales from my bench that I recount here are an eclectic bunch. There are obvious stories that you will hear on any walking tour of the city's sights that I don't even mention. As I said, this is not a guidebook. Instead, I have concentrated on those odd moments and small discoveries that have made me stop and think and that along the way allow me to paint a truer portrait of the city than any formal guide. As a scientist, who has concerned himself with discovery for many years, I have often found meaning and inspiration in what I have seen in Oxford. Equally, I have found puzzles and child-like wonder.

If you already know and love Oxford, perhaps you will hear these tales in the voice of an old friend — a kindred spirit; if you are a newcomer, or have yet to walk along Broad Street or peer through dark gateways into sunlit quads, then these stories may bring the city to life for you. Whatever the case, I hope you enjoy sitting on my bench as much as I have.

-1-
Oxford University Bench Press

People Watching and Listening on Broad Street

The sun is shining on my bench — and it is *my* bench, please make no mistake. Yes, I do allow others to use it, especially when I'm not actually in Oxford — I'm like that — but it is mine.

It sits, as I do now, in Broad Street, outside Balliol and Trinity, up from the White Horse Inn and opposite the red telephone box and the Information Centre. Placed right in the midst of things and with enough passers-by to merit the guides for the Oxford Walking Tour choosing it as their site to tout for business.

If you are on your way to the Bodleian Library, you pass my bench. If you are looking for coffee in Broad Street, you walk by me. If you want the Sheldonian Theatre, or Oxfam, or even if you are getting lost while trying to find the Ashmolean Museum you will stand puzzling before the tourist map on the board beside my bench.

Occasionally others come and sit beside me — to rest their legs or eat their lunch. I say nothing. I don't make a big thing about it being my bench and the fact that they haven't asked. I am magnanimous as I smile and move along to let them sit and make a mess with their sausage rolls from the bakery across the street.

From my bench I can see that it's a day of beginnings. It's moving in day at the start of Freshers' week. Improbably tall German students walk clutching their adapters newly bought to deal with fiendish English electricity, Chinese students pass carrying clothes horses in their polythene wrapping — one each. An American dad talks loudly to his embarrassed son, and everyone is carrying a duvet or a pillow or both. Larger than life luggage, bearing the tags for LHR, are rumbled across cobbles and street maps are clutched as close to hearts as dreams.

The traffic wardens, I note, are out in force today in Broad Street. Parking has never been easy in Oxford, but drivers are now given a harder time than ever. There are two wardens dressed in blue and white patrolling the couple of hundred metres of road before me. Moving like rather petulant magpies they are seeing what they can find. Not exactly two for joy.

A French couple and two Germans all speaking their own languages join me on the bench. Cosy. We are a little European Union in a line. I suspect the Germans are talking about the French and that the French are talking about me. In fact, I know they are — as I am familiar enough with their Gallic tongue to know that they have just wondered what the guy is writing. About you, *mes braves*. Unsafe to assume, I think, that French will not be understood in Oxford. You might be on safer ground with Serbo-Croat, Swedish even, but not French.

I sit soaking in the sun and half close my eyes to concentrate on the soundscape around me.

A couple of eager undergraduates stride past: 'Can condition be culturally defined?' she asks. 'No, my argument is...' he trails off as they move downwind to Blackwell's. 'That may well be,' says one older man who passes a younger one walking in the opposite direction. The latter saying to his perplexed companion, 'All I can say is that it was a fucking team effort.' 'Oh, is it your heel or part of your foot?' asks a rather concerned bohemian. Only to be crossed by two elderly men: 'Now, I wouldn't be saying this if it wasn't true,' one stage whispers to the other. A rather earnest pair: 'In the context of the playwright, I don't feel at one with the narrative.' 'Hhhh, hhhh, hhhh, hhhh...,' jogging by. Quizzically, 'you mean as opposed to being a small animal.' And, 'Dad, there's a naked man overseeing Broad Street.'

The naked man in question is made of bronze and because the sculptor Anthony Gormley has placed him on the roofline above Blackwell's Art Shop, he is indeed 'overseeing' the street. And he is indeed naked — prominently so.

The world flows by in both directions before my bench and I begin to feel that probably over time everybody who was anybody has walked by this spot. Albert Einstein on his way to his lecture, Robert Boyle rushing home to write his Law and even C.S. Lewis on his way to Narnia. Students and tourists and ordinary folk retrace the steps of the great, breathing the same air, feeling the same sun on their faces and saying probably exactly the same things across the generations. Everything changes while, of course, nothing changes at all.

And me — I'm still sitting on my bench in Broad Street, but there's room for a small one on the end if you want, for, although it is *my* bench, I don't mind sharing.

-2-
Coffee amongst the Spokes

Zappi's the Bike Shop Café

'You will need to have a love of great coffee, confidence in dealing with all sorts of people and a big tolerance of very sweaty people in Lycra'. Thus states the 'Help' ad on the wall of Zappi's, the eclectic, even by Oxford standards, café on St. Michael's Street. Here, amongst a low hanging forest of bicycle wheels and framed cycle jerseys, you can enjoy an Italian coffee or a loose leaf tea with freshly toasted banana bread that melts like a milkshake in the mouth. In truth, the counter staff do need some new help as they are rather more decorous than functional, but the ambience more than makes up for their youthful torpor.

Enter the bike shop and go up-rickety-stairs — the L-shaped flight has been adapted to include a narrow ramp for bringing bikes up — and you will find yourself in a café. Bright, beamed and brick-painted white it is crowded with the kind of Oxford life you would expect in such a choice corner. Students pore over their laptops and a couple of bearded dons discuss a little more loudly than is necessary the situation in Eastern Europe. In one corner an essay is being crafted and in another a hand is being caressed to seek forgiveness for something that happened the night before.

The combination of bicycle repair shop and café may at first appear incongruous, but like many such marriages of opposites it works rather wonderfully — fitting together, sharing a space and creating synergy where before there was simply the commonplace. There are other bike shops in the town and there are certainly many other cafés, but Zappi's is a little special and it is a better café as a result and, I expect, a better bike shop too.

Oxford is good at synergy and has long since realised that it is more than the basic sum of its parts. It places the old and the new side by side with architectural and cultural ease; honeyed stone abuts modern reinforced concrete and rolled lawn transitions into meadow; town meets gown and youth everywhere jostles with those old enough to know better. And whenever it does so, it creates a new experience, with more energy and verve than might be imagined.

Zappi's makes you think because a café in a bike shop is such a rich metaphor for some of the really good things in life. The juxtaposition of the unexpected makes both so much better than they would have been on their own. I once went to an American cinema where they served pizza slices during the show. I don't really remember the movie and I suspect the pizza was not in itself that special, but the experience of the two together remains vivid in my imagination. Just before Christmas I visited our local Children's Hospital and outside the main door was a pen containing several live reindeer complete with antlers and their handlers. I had seen reindeer before but to find them welcoming sick children and their parents to hospital a few days before they were due to pull Santa's sleigh suddenly moved me to tears. And of course in science, some of the greatest discoveries have been the result of the links made between the ordinary to create the extraordinary. The very act of creation is of course exactly that — the fusion of the commonplace, the crafting of the new. Creation is not magic, although it certainly sometimes looks like it from a distance. Rather it is a discovery of the joined up in a box of parts, none of which in themselves seem especially interesting. But the newly connected — the joined up — can take us by surprise.

I decide to order another coffee. I am eager to stay a little longer at the table in my metaphor for creativity, hopeful that a little more would rub off on me. At the left of the counter, however, I notice the chalk board.

One of Zappi's features, I learn, is their 'Treat a friend' board where you can pay in advance for a coffee and leave it with a chalked message on the board for a friend. When they next come in and find this simple act of kindness they can claim their drink, and perhaps leave one in return for their benefactor. All built on a special kind of trust, 'Latte for Oli' and 'Flat white for Miranda' could of course be redeemed by anyone, but the young woman behind the counter assures me, a little shocked at my suggestion of the potential for coffee fraud, that 'it all works very well.' I explain that I am from Glasgow, but she looks unimpressed and not really ready to forgive. I wonder momentarily if I should offer to caress her hand, but think better of it and continue on my way.

-3-

An Abundance of Absurdity

Oxford Rituals and Traditions

On Cornmarket Street, there is a man dressed as a large white rabbit who is riding a stationery penny-farthing bicycle while a bubble machine is filling the air around him. There is no performance other than his gentle waving to the crowd. On the river, opera singers in evening dress have just floated by, while signing at full blast to their audience of four in a punt. Upstairs in McDonalds, a town cryer with his 18th century dress and tricorn hat is sitting beside me having an Egg McMuffin for breakfast. And today the emperors' heads outside the Science Museum are wearing specs.

There is an oddness to the sights and sounds of Oxford that borders on the absurd. But it is an absurdity worn with a certain pride — perhaps even disdain. Today, Oxford clearly savours its originality and its sense of uniqueness, but the abundance of its absurdity has its origins in its University's rituals and traditions, developed over an 800 year history.

There are almost too many of these to enumerate and when you first arrive in Oxford and hear its students talk, you can be baffled by a vocabulary that you are unlikely to hear elsewhere. Formal Halls and High Tables, Bedels and Battels, Convocation, Rustication and Supplication as well as Scholars, Exhibitioners and Commoners, and Michaelmas, Hilary and Trinity. As you delve into University life you will also discover a world that is governed by ritual and organised by tradition — a world that any new student quickly either relishes or finds too silly for words.

Tom Tower, the mighty stone bastion above the gateway to Christ Church College, bears the clock that tells Oxford time — five minutes behind Greenwich Mean Time — and at 9.00pm (or rather 9.05pm) its bell tolls not nine times but a hundred and one times imposing its curfew on its 100 members. One new member was added in 1664, necessitating the extra chime.

At certain times of the year you will see worried looking students in their subfusc (formal black and white clothing) and black gowns making their concentrated way towards the University's Examination Schools on High Street. Pinned to their gowns some will have carnations to denote that they are sitting finals, and the colour of the flower is a code for whether it is their first exam (white), a middle exam (pink) or the last (red).

Twice a year, crews of eight in their long, narrow and rather flimsy looking boats vie to be *Head of the River*. The river in question is the Thames before it flows on into London, but here it is called the Isis. Not you might presume after the Egyptian goddess, but a simple abbreviation of the Latin name for the river — *Tamesis*. As the river here is too narrow for two boats to race against each other, side by side, Oxford has developed a peculiar competition known as Bumps. As the name implies boats chase each other with the intention of catching the boat in front and escaping the one behind. Over four days in early spring and early summer the winner of the Bumps can claim that coveted title, Head of the River.

And Blues. There is, as you might expect, intense rivalry between Oxford and, as they call it here, 'the other place' that the rest of us call Cambridge, the other great seat of learning in England. *Cantabrigiensis* is Latin for *of Cambridge* and is routinely abbreviated to *Cantab* after a degree to signify a graduate's alma mater. Cantab is, however, further mutilated by Oxford students to the derogatory *Tabs* as a name for their rivals. That rivalry, as well as being academic, finds its most tangible form in the arena of sport, where Oxford makes every attempt to 'shoo the Tabs' or beat Cambridge. There are over seventy sports competed by Oxford and Cambridge and these are known as varsity matches. Fifty of these sports carry full blue or half blue status. The University colour of both Oxford and Cambridge is, conveniently, blue — Oxford, dark blue and Cambridge, light. Winners of these matches may be awarded a Blue and be given the right, some would say distinction, of wearing a blues blazer as a badge of honour. Blues are thus highly sought after for they look as good on the CV as a first class honours degree.

Traditions are the mortar that holds the honeyed stones of Oxford together. They can be the objects of derision for some, providing all the evidence needed for the charge of elitism. Archaic and deliberately arcane, these traditions are explicitly designed to separate and divide us into those who know and those who don't. On the other hand they can be embraced as part of the magic of this academic theme park. They can be seen as the tangible evidence of our links with the past; with a lineage of scholarship that continues unbroken across eight centuries. Students today wear their gowns with pride and live in walled colleges as did their forefathers, some of whom were novelists, poets, architects, scientists, prime ministers, presidents and kings — all of whom wore their carnations, watched the bumps and dreamed of blues.

Conformity to a new and altogether strange set of norms allows new, and perhaps frightened, students to find a community and at the same time it serves to reinforce that feeling of Dorothy's — that they are assuredly 'no longer in Kansas.'

Students, for the most part, are young and eager to be different. While there are exotic fashions, technicolored hairstyles and piercings galore there are also essays being written in cafés and thick books being read on lawns. Everywhere there is an undercurrent of study and industry for this cohort, the latest to grace the colleges of Oxford, know exactly what they have and just how hard it was to get it. Still, they will try to shock, but Oxford has dealt with millions of students and it knows it will still be here when they are gone — long gone.

And that white rabbit on the bike? Oxford walks by, without batting an eyelid. In 800 years it's seen it all before, and it's not even its first white rabbit.

-4-

Einstein's Blackboard

Museum of the History of Science

The floors creak with age and the weight of importance, for what rests preserved behind glass in the modern display cases has a fair chance of taking your breath away. Climb the stairs in front of the History of Science Museum in Oxford's Broad Street just across from the White Horse Inn and you will find yourself in the building that was the original home of the Ashmolean Museum.

Built in 1683, the Old Ashmolean claims to be the world's oldest surviving purpose-built museum.   When the Ashmolean outgrew this space and moved across town to its now much more lavish residence, adjacent to the Randolph Hotel, the original building was put to several uses, most recently becoming a dedicated space to showcase science.

Although small, the museum offers such a range of possibilities that it is difficult to pick a favourite. The exhibits range from the simple, through to the odd and on up the scale to the magical, arriving finally at the awesome. You will find brass microscopes and ivory slide rules. You will find the crafted components of physics and chemistry laboratories and evidence of Oxford's role in the development of penicillin. In the 1940s, starved of resources, but not resourcefulness, Florey and Chain resorted to using old metal biscuit tins as their culture flasks. That work led to the commercially viable production of the first antibiotic and you will find their tins stacked as they left them. Look further and you will even find an exquisitely engraved confection from the 16th century, that probably still bears the royal fingerprints of its owner, for this is the astrolabe of Queen Elizabeth I. And, if you look up, you will find Einstein's blackboard.

It is hard not to be impressed by Einstein's blackboard. It hangs above eye-level sealed behind glass, but the chalked equations are as crisp and fluid as the day they were written more than 80 years ago. Not having a mathematical bone in my body, I did not know what was being proved, but I didn't really care, for this was not only Einstein's handwriting, this was tangible evidence of his thought.

Einstein was already a physics superstar because of his special and general theories of relativity when he was invited to lecture in Oxford in 1931. He gave three lectures on relativity, doubtless to rapt audiences, and from the second of these, the black board he used has been preserved.

You can imagine the thoughts of the organisers in the front row, when the lecture was over. Thinking that the great man's work should be preserved they were probably nervous. As Einstein was taking questions from the audience, he might at any moment casually pick up the duster and wipe away their little piece of history. But, perhaps they didn't need to worry as Einstein at this stage in his illustrious career was probably not used to wiping his own boards.

They took it down, sealed it and put it on display, but why? I suspect they had in mind my intake of breath when I first saw it. They knew that I, like so many others who would never hear or meet Albert Einstein in person, could find themselves in his presence by standing in front of his writing. Writing that is clearly readable, simply formed, and framed by his chain of connected thought. Einstein is one of those scientists who has entered mythology, becoming in the process the stereotype of the tousled professor. He has transcended his Nobel Prize and found his way to his seat in popular culture.

But now, in front of his blackboard, the mythology melts away and the dazzling mind of a physicist who tackled time and space is revealed. It is very hard not to gulp, ever so slightly. I stood back for a moment and watched others walk by. Each would peruse the glass cases and then, almost by accident, glance up. Not sure what they were looking at, they would consult the small description to the side, look again and mouth their silent wows.

Celebrity in science is, for the most part, a bad thing. Scientists should really be defined by their work and we should care less for the man or woman behind the ideas. Of course, that's not the way it works. We are fascinated by Marie Curie's family life, by Isaac Newton's nervous breakdowns and Albert Einstein's dislike of haircuts. Surnames become chemical elements and SI units offering immortality, when it's the ideas that should be immortal or at least kept alive just as long as they are needed.

We have a human need, however, to connect with the humanity of our stars, whether in science or elsewhere and one obvious way to do this is to share their space. We place our hands in their cement impressions, we marvel at their costumes, and in the case of Einstein we trace his writing with our eyes and open mouths.

Einstein left Oxford, but he left his chalk marks behind. I suspect he did not anticipate his mathematics would still be hanging on a wall more than 50 years after his death, but I was grateful that they were. I was thankful to those organisers who a lifetime ago had placed his blackboard safely out of duster reach, so that we could all, at least for a few moments, attend Einstein's lecture on relativity.

And, in case you are wondering what the equations are actually about, the small sign beside the exhibit helpfully states, 'The first three lines establish an equation for D, the measure of expansion in the universe. The lower four lines provide numerical values for the expansion, density, radius and age of the universe.' Of course they do.

-5-
Taking a Punt

The River Cherwell

'Shall we go punting?' These were words I never thought I would hear. I'm from Glasgow, you understand. That they should come out of the mouth of my son made the incredulity that much more acute. I suppose when my son went to Oxford I should have expected that this day might come, but I was frankly unprepared. I had no white linen suit, no panama hat, no champagne picnic in a wicker basket and Lord Sebastian Flyte with that naughty teddy bear, Aloysius, were nowhere to be seen.

It was, however, a sunny autumn afternoon with the willows brushing the waters of the Cherwell and I had to agree. The punt was hired, the seat cushions, paddle and pole collected, and as my son was going to be doing the actual punting, all I had to do was get into the boat. There may be a better illustration of Newton's laws of motion than the inexperienced trying to board a punt, but I'm not sure what it might be. 'Every action has an equal and opposite reaction,' roughly translates as: you step forward and the punt goes backwards, and, unless you flail around to recover your balance and your dignity, you end up in the river.

With some hilarity, what seemed like the impossible was finally achieved and I was seated and breathless on the newly positioned cushions. It seemed best that I should be recumbent. My son, a physicist, explained something about centres of gravity that went over my head, so I lay still, trying to be a sleeping dog. He took charge of the pole, and having done this before, pushed off with some aplomb and in seconds we floated away.

It was a silent, seductive way to travel, with gentle ripples on the bow and the rhythm of the pole sliding down through open hands into the water, the push and then the pull of it through the river steering the punt as an extended rudder, before repeating the move. There was a paddle, which I started to use in an attempt to assist his pole-action, but I was asked to desist, as whichever side of the punt I choose to paddle on was driving him off course.

My efforts unappreciated, I decided to relax and soak up the experience. There was the glitter of sunlight through willow leaves, a gentle breeze on the water and some coots by the riverbank. And, there were other punts. There is a camaraderie amongst punters. We were all gliding together. We were all grateful to be enjoying the sunshine and the river. And, we were all feeling just a little bit special and a little bit smug. We smiled at each other as we passed. Perhaps a wave, a nod and an occasional word.

'We're finished with these ducks. Would you like them?' asked one punt passenger surrounded by hungry ducks while holding an empty bag of breadcrumbs.

'Stop at the pub. The punting's much easier after a drink, or two,' advised a reclining puntee. Red plastic champagne flute in hand, this languid lady raised her 'glass' in acknowledgement and glided on.

Iridescent headed mallards kept pace with us. Looking to be fed, they paddled alongside and once they had confirmed our cupboard was bare, squawked (ducks don't really quack do they?) and went off to find another, more accommodating, punt.

Just as I was beginning to think that I could probably live like this for the rest of my life, I was asked the second question of the day that I never expected to hear. 'Would you like to learn how to punt, Dad?' Now, being a passenger was one thing, but taking the helm, or at least the pole, was another. Especially, as it would inevitably mean both standing up and having to tackle Newton and his laws all over again. But, it was clear that if I did not say yes, I would never be asked again. I smiled, stood up, made my way to the Oxford end of the boat, took my son's place and quickly acquired mastery of the 5m long aluminium pole.

Well, that's what it will look like in the film of my life. The reality was considerably more wobbly, hesitant, funny, ridiculous and fumbling. But, despite the comedy, I did get there, and although I steered us into the bank twice and got a lot of the river up my sleeve, I did not fall in and I did get the hang of both the propulsion and the steering. And, I am a little ashamed to say, I felt rather proud of myself.

It is surprising how rarely we learn new skills as an adult. As a child, an adolescent and as a student acquiring new skills is the norm. Then, after the hurly-burly of education we settle into a life that often lacks — how should I put it — the freshness of the new. Someone once told me that to fend off senility I should learn how to play a new musical instrument and how to speak a new foreign language every year. This seemed like rather a tall order to me, but I did accept the wisdom of the sentiment. We need to learn new things, acquire new skills, stretch and challenge ourselves in order to stay alive. Sometimes all it takes is the abandon to say, 'yes'.

I could have sat in a cafe that afternoon with my son, but I already knew how to drink coffee. I could have pored over the weekend newspaper, but I already knew how to read. I could have strolled along the riverbank, but I already knew how to walk. On the other hand, saying yes, allowed me to get a little wet, a little muddy and to learn something new and much more important.

What did I learn? That, most assuredly, you can teach an old (Scottish) dog new tricks. And it was magical.

-6-
Fragment of a Royal Nose

The Ashmolean Museum

The rain was battering against the windows of the Ashmolean Museum so hard that the place was becoming positively rowdy. Normally hushed hallways of statuary were transformed by drum rolls of weather and a horde of wet visitors escaping from the rain. Like many others we had dripped our way through the oversized glass revolving door and into the entrance hall, and then turning left to find some space had found ourselves in 'Nubia and Ancient Egypt'. Time and place transformed in the turn of a corner, we marvelled at hieroglyphic strewn tombs and funerary goods by the display case load. However, what caught my attention, and held it, was not some beautifully carved alabaster figurine or a delicately painted coffin lid, but a knobbly piece of stone about the size of a decent sized bread bin that hung on the wall.

I looked and puzzled and wondered: was it an Ancient Egyptian meteorite or perhaps a misplaced exhibit from the geology section? There may have been some man-made marks on it, but I couldn't be certain. The small panel describing it was not placed directly beneath it and I wondered if I was reading the correct label, especially when it said: 'Fragment of a Royal Nose.'

Well. My first thought, I must admit, was, 'what a good title for a novel.' Then, I started to think. How do they know it's a nose? There might be some nostrils, or equally there might not be and as to its provenance being Royal, well that seemed frankly supposition. Mind you it was on the large side. If this was the nose, or more correctly a fragment of the nose, the face by my reckoning of this presumptive royal would have been about 2m from top to bottom. If the face was attached to a body, we were probably in the realm of half the height of the Statue of Liberty.

The label further defined the lump as the quartzite nose of King Amenemhat III from about 1844-1797 BC. That is, a 3800 year old nose. It also said the nose was from a seated figure — not quite so high then.

But, my problem was this. What is a lump of rock that gives no real indication of what it is, who made it, how it was made, why or when it was made doing as an exhibit in one of the world's great museums? We have to take for granted the word of the curator when we view most items in a museum, but this fragment of stone required greater suspension of disbelief than usual. If you had told me this rock had been recovered from the Sea of Tranquility, from the walls of Jericho or that it had come from the depths of the ocean I would be just as likely to believe or disbelieve you as I would be when asked to accept that it was a royal nose - or a fragment thereof.

So, what's this all about? If all you have is a fragment with a ropey provenance then that's what you have to put on show, or it has to stay in the box. I am sure the Ashmolean curators would have loved to have had the whole nose, but they just didn't and that's that. They made do. Time to ponder the key question. Is a fragment of a royal nose better or worse than no nose at all? I am inclined, having studied the fragment in question, to conclude that something is always better than nothing. This rather battered relic had already stopped me in my tracks. Intact mummy cases and grave goods were waiting to be viewed, but they have been put on hold in favour of a fragment. The partial, you see, allows imagination to fill in the gaps. This relic was quickly assuming the proportions of a colossus; its story revealed to an open mind with closed eyes. The ancient sands of Egypt part and a mighty pharaoh sits carved in time. Almost four millennia pass and the pharaoh is unseated and shattered by war and siege and plunder. His countenance erased, broken for building materials and used again and again through the years. Then, a mere century ago, an Oxford archaeologist stumbles upon a fragment and brings it home to a gaslit study. Now, refurbished and burnished and mounted, the royal stone hangs on the wall of a new gallery in an old museum. And all this from a broken piece of masonry. Well, actually, no. All this from a small card placed under a lump of unrecognisable, gnarled stoned that claims the exhibit as a 'Fragment of a Royal Nose.'

The story is everything. The romance of the imponderably old that conjures the cavalcade of history comes from the story, not the thing itself. The splinter of bone, the scrap of leather, the shard of pottery. In themselves, these are nothing, but when we hear of the warrior's shattered skull, the long-bowman's quiver or the drinking vessel of a long-dead queen we believe so much more than we can see. The architecture of our own wonder is evidence of our need to discover and to imagine what might yet be discovered. We can build flights of fancy based on the merest of suggestion. But, it is this same facility that allows us to see in a grain of sand the stuff of stars.

Wonder is at the heart of our discovery, and imagination is its soul. In science, our discoveries are as hard won as any of the trophies of archaeology, and any fragments of knowledge we uncover should be similarly displayed with pride, to tantalise, and fuel the search for the whole.

-7-
Compline by Candlelight

Exeter College Chapel

At dusk Oxford bustles. Workers return home, shoppers wait for buses and students bike their way around the narrow side streets. And bells tend to toll. On such an evening, the spire of the chapel of Exeter College on Broad Street was amber lit from within creating a fireside glow in the sky and choristers dressed in Lenten black waited in the quadrangle outside. An unbeliever, I was unsure of my welcome, but it was warm as I entered, tentatively, the glittering sanctum of the Chapel for the evening service of Compline.

This was the last service of the day for the medieval monks and served as a completion to their day of rhythmic toil and worship. More out of curiosity than devotion, I decided to attend the service when I spotted the poster for it earlier in the day. My day in Oxford had been filled with thoughtful strolls, quiet inspiration and the much appreciated opportunity to sit and think and write. My head was busy with the thoughts and sights of the previous hours and Compline seemed an appropriate way to end my day too.

The chapel like all those of Oxford colleges was grander and more opulent that you might expect. Neo-gothic architecture, lavish stained glass, highly polished brass and candlelight. The mellow light softened the stone and, flickering, caught the gold in the mosaics above the altar creating an impression of slight movement in the figures of the ancient saints.

The congregation was surprisingly sparse. I counted thirteen including myself and I wondered why people would not be flocking to such a stage to hear the singing of the student choir. And what singing. Plainsong chants followed by the soaring voices of Bruckner's Christus Factus Est. I defy anyone, regardless of their faith or lack of it, not to be moved and affected by what I heard.

The service was designed to appeal to all the senses. The polished and highly carved end-rails on the seats felt like exotic fruits to the touch. The smoking censor swung from adept hands and filled the chapel with Eastern scents. The beauty of the carved stone and colourful mosaics wrapped around us creating a visual feast in the candleglow. But most of all there was the sound.

At times you had to close your eyes to limit the sensory overload, just to concentrate on the unutterably beautiful fusion of male and female voices lifting and soaring into the vaulted ceiling and reverberating around.

Despite my lack of faith in any god, I found much to be thankful for in the service. And it was about giving thanks for the gifts of the day. Gratitude sung as well as sensed. This scented sanctuary at dusk also offered a chance for reflection at the end of a day. Thoughts of what had gone before and what was yet to come found a place between the music and the prayer. A reading from the book of Isaiah was lost upon me, but gave me the chance to lose myself in the archaic word forms — the 'wherefores' and the 'thous' circled around my ears and hypnotised me. I heard none of what, I suppose, I was expected to hear, but what I did hear were my own thoughts.

Meditation and the mindfulness of the moment are important, perhaps essential, in this ever expanding life we lead. Stopping and looking at the candle flame, examining your thoughts, experiencing the sensation of being alive, of breathing a perfumed air and of hearing just what human voices can do.

All this held me in the moment for as long as I was in the chapel. As I left, the College Chaplain took my hand to shake it, looked into my eyes and thanked me for sharing in the Compline service. I was too overwhelmed to correct him — it was I who should be thanking him and his choir and the 2000 years of history and devotion that had led to this night. I suddenly also felt the urge to apologise for my lack of faith and to admit my shady status as an imposter. But, just as suddenly, I realised as I looked back at him that this was all unnecessary. The welcome I had received was not only warm, it was unconditional. I went out into the now dark night air, which carried just a hint of Spring warmth. The bustle in the streets had subsided a little and so had my thoughts. I felt calm and gave quiet thanks to the night.

-8-
Let Curiosity Lead the Way

The Pitt-Rivers Museum

Visiting the Pitt-Rivers Museum in Oxford is rather like clambering through the attic of an eccentric uncle. The word cornucopia could have been coined to describe this confusion of riches from across the globe, housed in the dimly lit, Victorian warehouse adjoining the Natural History Museum in Oxford.

Tightly packed glass cases vie for your attention. As you bend over carefully examining the objects in one display case, you only become aware of the objects above your head — spears, paddles, kites and objects from every time and culture that defy identification — because of their reflection in the glass.

'Don't miss the *Shrunken Heads*,' I was advised. I stumbled upon them and gazed like everyone else at the grotesques that had once been the faces of men and women. I wondered if it would be a sacrilege or an honour to be preserved in such a way and to spend eternity on open display. An immortality of a sort, but a nameless one. You cannot wonder for long, for behind you is the history of writing, to one side of you the development of trumpets and along the narrow aisle, as much as you would care to know about weaving practices around the world.

The Pitt-Rivers Museum starts to hurt in a physical way. There is too much and you are overwhelmed. 'Is this your first visit, sir?' asked a smiling attendant. He had clearly seen many visitors advance through the stages of awe, wonder and then despair that my face had been exhibiting. 'Perhaps, you would like a floor plan — we have several levels and there is no start or finish or planned route to follow, but we encourage you to wander and let your curiosity lead you.' I was not entirely sure my curiosity was up to the task, but I nodded, took the floor plan and thanked him. I decided to escape the confusion of the ground floor and gain a higher vantage point on one of the floors above to survey and map out my plan of attack. That, however, proved fruitless. From above the museum seemed even larger and if anything more crowded with artefacts crammed to bursting into old glass cases everywhere I looked. Where to begin?

I am more used to the modern approach to museums where a defined route, signposted by numbered, well-spaced, well-lit exhibits. This was certainly not that; this was about as far from that as it was possible to get. I felt as if I was in a bazaar or a flea market with particularly good items for sale. I half expected to be accosted by haggling traders as I turned the corner from *Body Art* into *Feather Headdresses*. But, no this was a museum, with nothing for sale but knowledge and the price of that was merely wonder. I decided I would have to follow the attendant's instruction and let my curiosity guide the way. I glanced and dwelt and moved on. As colours caught my eye, I paused and smiled. I realised that I would have to relinquish any notion of seeing it all. Indeed, I found it hard to imagine that even those in charge knew of everything they had or that any accurate inventory had ever been compiled.

But, I didn't need to see it all to start enjoying it. I was led on a meandering walk between cases and all that led me was a desire to see what was next. Surprise after surprise fed my curiosity, whose appetite seemed unsatisfied by such a banquet. This was truly an all you can eat buffet of world culture, but curiosity seems to become hungrier the more it is fed. The couple of hours I had allowed myself in the museum passed quickly and I left stimulated but also recognised the need for a return visit, for many return visits. Our curiosity is so central to the business of discovery. Without it, we can never wonder why or how or what if, and the research questions that we must carefully define can never be born. For curiosity to thrive it must be fed. It is hard to imagine that great ideas have occurred to minds locked in grey rooms with no sight of the sky. So, we must go out of our way to nourish our imaginations and watch as it hungers for more.

As I left, a sign above the door caught my eye. It was a carved plaque with the words of William Morris: 'We are only trustees for those who come after us.' The collectors who had assembled the myriad of objects in the Pitt-Rivers Museum, and indeed every museum, knew that. They knew that they were feeding the minds of the next generation, to whom they entrusted their collections. In turn, we tend their legacy, adding to it, ready to pass on to the next. As long as there are museums, our curiosities will be well-fed and equally hungry for more.

-9-
The Erasure of Memory
St. Mary Magdalen's Church Yard

Between the daffodils and the last of the crocuses, the sandstone memorials stand slightly stooped with age. Leaning forwards or to the side they mark the resting places of the long dead, but marking is all they can now do for age has not only wearied them, but worn away all trace of their memorial. Nameless and dateless, these sad stones stand vigil in the church yard of St. Mary Magdalen on Oxford's Magdalen Street.

Forgotten, the dead are erased from their headstones by the elements. Layer by layer the stones are peeled apart by the same forces of nature that formed them in the first place, long before they ever found their place in a church yard. Wind and rain and time have done their inevitable work. For such a brief moment in their geological history these stones carried the name of the person who was once the body buried beneath them, but all too soon they have returned to the anonymity they had known for millennia before and will know for the remaining years to come. The people beneath them existed for a fraction of the life of their headstones and all trace of them is now gone, even though stone seemed, in comparison to their fragile lives, such a permanent reminder of their existence.

We memorialise to remember. Those we have lost we hold in our memories; keeping them alive in our thoughts. As time passes and the pain of bereavement is blunted, we may be disturbed to realise that some of the details are slipping away. Like a fading photograph in the sun the definition goes and the image is softened and finally lost. Headstones offer loved ones the false reassurance of permanence. A resting place is marked forever and some of the heavy work of remembrance will be taken from our shoulders. Stone, however, as we can see in this church yard, is only a short term solution, lasting a few hundred years at most. But, that's more than enough for most. Memories die with us and few of us live on in the remembrance of more than one or two generations.

For some, however, the legacy of memory is the hallmark of success. A life memorialised, or perhaps more importantly, a life's work remembered, is to some all that really matters. When we think of the great who have gone before, we sometimes have tangible evidence that they lived and that they breathed the same air as us. Museums are filled with the paraphernalia of lives gone by — the gloves worn by a princess, the spectacles worn by a scientist, the lock of hair of an author — but these are insignificant in comparison to the thoughts and ideas that these people left behind. Ideas can, and do, change lives. They move worlds and shape futures and live on long after the flesh has rotted from our bones and even our headstones have regressed into anonymous slabs.

But for ideas to survive they must be recorded and documented, and the written word has proved more permanent than any stone to pass a memory down through the ages. We know what philosophers and kings thought because of what they wrote, or what has been written about them. We know of discoveries ancient and modern because they have been shared in the scientific literature and now sit on our library shelves. The works of dead scientists are there to be read and climbed upon that we might see just that little bit further than them. And we know how timeless our human emotions are because they have been written about in much the same ways for thousands of years by countless story tellers. Songs of love and sorrow, joy and heartache, jealously and rage fill the scrolls of ancient sagas just as they do the pages of any Hollywood script today.

The words of all these writers are their headstones, unweathered by rain, spoken sometimes across centuries, yet still heard, still listened to, still making a difference.

Most of St. Mary Magdalen's stones are worn and weathered, but one small headstone near the iron railing that encloses the church yard is now completely covered in ivy. Whether the name is still there beneath this mound of overgrowth is impossible to see. While it is tempting to part the leaves to reveal who lies beneath, to do so, however, feels unseemly. This stone is in effect veiled. Just as the forces of nature have erased the names on the other stones, another force of nature — life itself — has chosen to obscure this one from view. The dead in St. Mary Magdalen's sleep on anonymous. Their identities, like ours one day, may be lost, but not necessarily their thoughts. These can live on in the memory of the written word.

-10-
Dinosaurs in Bubble Wrap

The Natural History Museum Part 1

If you ever have to renovate your Natural History Museum, you will have to deal with the same set of challenges currently faced by Oxford. As their Great Hall is shrouded in scaffolding and shuttering, there are some things you just can't move. Larger skeletons and, of course, your dinosaurs. To protect them from the ravages, not of time but of plaster dust, falling scaffolding clamps and even any errant power tool, you need to wrap them. Or re-wrap them to be more accurate. All fossils have, after all, spent the majority of their existence encased in the earth. As faithful reproductions of bones and shells and leaves crystallised in the rock they become part of what they have lain hidden within — wrapped and entombed in history.

These particular fossils were released by ardent Victorians with little rock hammers and big ambitions, and have now spent a very brief time adorning the walls and halls of the museum. Now, even more briefly, they are put back to sleep, blanketed in bubble wrap and hidden again from sight. In so doing, they re-acquire a little of their former mystery, their labels now removed and their form again unsure. They also become works of modern art rather than specimens of palaeontology, glacial in their iced wrappings. In their present form they could be the work of Damien Hirst and would not look out of place in a New York gallery. The bubble wrap also does something else: it fleshes out their naked fossil bones and gives these lumbering giants a bulk they only had in life. For all these reasons I decided I rather preferred my dinosaurs wrapped.

But, of course it made me think, for that's what museums are for. There was something intriguing about the notion of first carefully releasing an ancient animal from the rock only to encase it in plastic: painstakingly revealing and then concealing, in sequence. There was a metaphor there for our business of discovery and our subsequent obfuscation of science.

In science, we spend many hours carefully chipping away in order to reveal the truth; to satisfy ourselves that we have the complete artefact, the whole story. Like the fossilised bone of a dinosaur our scientific truth finally lies bare and revealed for all to see. However, what we then do is rewrap our discovery in a language that serves to conceal it. As professional scientists we have been taught the words we must use to describe and interpret our discoveries. We write our papers and publish them in cryptic journals, read only by a privileged few who are in the know — part of the club. There is no attempt made, nor any expected, to share these discoveries with the wider scientific community or indeed the public. Science has indeed become a very closed shop. The words we use and the media we choose to convey them make sure our dinosaur bones are well wrapped and hidden from anyone but the cognoscenti.

In effect, we bubble wrap our ideas just as the museum protects its bones. Our discoveries are sealed in plastic to protect them from the gaze of those outside our field, cushioned against the troubling touch of others. What we revealed is now, at least partially, re-hidden. Modern science has thus become a highly specialised affair. Never mind the public, this obfuscation means that even a scientist from one field has little access to the discoveries on one in another.

This may seem to be an inevitable consequence of the depth to which we now take our personal interests, but it forces us to work in subject silos. Of course, it would be fanciful to imagine that we could return to the days when we believed it was possible to know everything, and the enlightened gentleman (the enlightened gentlewomen rarely got a look in) could afford to be interested in everything. Now, we are specialists by necessity, but it is important to recognise the possibilities that exist at the edges of our subject where they abut on to our neighbours' land. The most beautiful flowers, it is said, grow at the edges of the garden because of the possibilities of cross fertilization — two goods combining to make a wonderful. If we have lost the ability to share our ideas and our findings with those outside our field, or if, worse, we think it unimportant to do so, we are seriously missing a trick. To communicate our work we need to break free of the constraints taught to us by our mentors. We need to learn to share our ideas in language that will inspire as well as inform without the bubble wrap of overly technical language and what amounts to plain old jargon. Only then will our dinosaurs be there for the viewing

All wrapped up they may be mysterious, and they may even be strangely beautiful, but what they are not is accessible. And, access may be everything.

-11-
The Fox and the Meteorite

The Natural History Museum Part 2

'Noses against glass,' is the way we are asked to study most exhibits in a museum. We can see them but we cannot touch them, and for good reasons. A thousand fingerprints a day would soon disintegrate many artefacts and museums are as much about preservation as they are about display. But being separated from an object does have its disadvantages and we all have a childlike desire to handle when we are told we can only look.

Some museums have decided to cater to this deep-seated need and, perhaps in order to preserve everything else in their collections from groping hands, they have identified a small number of exhibits that sit on tables with labels that say, 'Please Touch'. These labels always have to be looked at twice just to make sure and even then most people are still a little furtive when they start to handle the objects on the touch table.

Confronted with such a display, I, like most people, hesitated. I began with an object that had already been through so much trauma that I doubted I could add to its woes with some gentle touch.

The meteorite, I was informed by its label, was from Argentina. They meant, of course, that it fell to earth there for I suspect it was *from* considerably further afield. At 4.6 billion years old it was probably the oldest object I would ever touch. And touch it I did. It felt not like rock, but like sculpted bronze; cold and crafted into an abstract form with indentations that almost formed finger holes for my hand. Its journey had been long and heated, finally hurtling through our nascent atmosphere to find its way to land that would one day become the continent of South America, but was probably a long way yet from its present position in the Southern Hemisphere.

Emboldened by my success with the meteorite, I decided to try another object. In contrast to the hardness and coldness of the meteorite, the fox on the other hand, quite literally, was soft and warm. I had seen many foxes darting in the dark across roads, their eyes caught in my headlights, their long brush tails pulled behind them into the hedgerows. But, here before me in broad daylight was an adult vixen, long dead and stuffed, but no less beautiful. She sat with her long black trimmed ears alert, wearing her red fox fur coat and her luxuriant brush wrapped around her hind legs. No glass separated us and I reached out to stroke her back. She did not feel stuffed and lifeless, but rather simply still. I then stroked her head and beneath her chin as I would a domestic dog. And then the white fur of her breast. None of these movements would of course be possible in life, at least not while retaining all five fingers.

Holding an ancient meteorite in your hand and being able to stroke a fox are normally disallowed. To do so was not only exciting it was also a little unnerving. Like catching a glimpse of something that shouldn't be seen, overhearing a private conversation, or even reading someone else's letter, there was a feeling on unease as well as just a little exhilaration. Here you were in a situation that was unnatural and that in the normal course of affairs would never be. But by being afforded this chance, the connections made through touch yield interesting emotions. A meteorite in a glass case is a dark misshapen lump that is easy to pass over. A meteorite in the hand conveys the silent coldness of space as well as the burning of its re entry. The birth of the universe is in your hand, not some geological specimen.

So too with the fox. These are pretty animals and rather interesting, but a stuffed lifeless specimen in a glass case is unlikely to rouse the spirit. Place it before you, however, take away the glass and allow yourself to caress its fur and draw the outlines of its pointed ears and its long tail with your fingers and it becomes an animal of rare beauty that you would no longer wish to see hunted or harmed.

Exposure, close up and very personal, is an acute form of education. No amount of words or pictures or specimens in glass cases will ever have the impact of the real thing in your hands. Experiences are what make education come alive, as all good teachers know, and any museum that tries this approach should be applauded. Of course, I understand that we can't all try on Tutankhamun's death mask, or handle the Magna Carta, or flick through the Dead Sea scrolls, but there are plenty of lesser objects that we could allow the young (and the not so young) to touch and experience. Why not start with the meteorites, and the foxes.

-12-
'It's later than you think...'

The Siew-Sngiem Clocktower & Sukum Navapan Gate, Harris Manchester College

As a lover of history, it is tempting to believe that everything in the past is better. Particularly, when it comes to craftsmanship, there is a widely held notion that it effectively ceased to exist sometime in the last 50 years. For example, we wander around cities and stare, awestruck by the beauty and artistry of the stonework on old buildings. At the same time we shake our heads, saddened that we can no longer achieve such finesse. But, reality is a little different from our perception — isn't it always? Have people changed, are we less skilled than our forebears, do we now care less about beauty and craft?

It would be easy and obvious to talk of the architectural grandeur of Oxford as a history lesson. The gargoyles of the Bodleian Library, the dome of the Radcliffe Camera, Tom Tower of Christ Church, the spires of Magdalen and St. Mary the Virgin, and the giant carved heads outside the Sheldonian Theatre. Collectively, all these are what makes Oxford so striking, especially to the first time visitor. Seven hundred years of building and sculpture laid out before you as a catalogue of the best that architecture had to offer. But, despite my love of history, I am not interested in the past for its own sake. I read and study history to inform the present — my present. Why is my world the way it is now? Why do people behave the way they do around me? Why do I feel and think the things I do? There are many places to look for such answers, but I choose to look, perhaps forensically, to the past. I look for causes to link with consequences in the hope that an understanding of the 'why' might help soften the blow of reality.

When an opportunity arises then to glimpse history in the making — to witness the creation of something that people are undoubtedly going to look back upon and wonder, I am naturally drawn to it. So, rather than focus on the old, let's look at something as new as it gets. Let's look at Oxford's latest building. At the corner of Holywell St and Mansefield Road, a new addition to Harris Manchester College is slowly being revealed. As the scaffolding comes down and the hoardings are removed the latest addition to the Oxford stonescape is, I think, majestically beautiful.

A new clock tower and gateway endowed by benefactors from Thailand in memory of their parents stands as vivid testimony against the case that craftsmanship is dead. The workmen creating the new gateway and clock tower are still at work in their hard hats and fluorescent hi-viz jackets as I stand and watch. They have tattoos and earrings and read the Sun — just like all craftsmen through the ages they do not regard themselves as special, but simply as working men doing a job. They are strong and unshaven and their talk is rough. But their work is smooth as polished stone as they carve Palladian finials and porticos and even an elephant's head from the yellow Oxford stone.

The octagonal tower they have fashioned carries five clock faces and time is the central theme here. We are reminded on one side of the tower that, 'It's later than you think...' Sobering, but softened by the riposte on the next side, which reassures us, '...but it is never too late'. Appropriate sentiments for a College that only admits mature students to study for undergraduate or postgraduate degrees. On top of it all is a playful weather vane showing a student on a bike, complete with flowing gown and mortar board rushing off in whatever direction the wind should take him.

A combination of designs old and new, the tower and gateway have been truly crafted and will stand for the next five hundred years slowly becoming part of historic Oxford, slowly contributing to the disappointment of future generations that we can no longer build beauty in stone the way they used to.

In a city like Oxford we are surrounded by architectural beauty because of workmen with hods and hammers, stonemasons and iron workers and architects with dreams. And they are still here, as they are everywhere. Beauty is not the prerogative of the past; nor is craftsmanship the hallmark of a time gone by. People are no different today than when they toiled over the great cathedrals of Europe or the grand avenues of our capital cites; when they built castles and palaces and memorials to the fallen. Our capacity to create the functional, the beautiful and the wondrous are undiminished. True, we often decide that we can no longer afford such beauty, but that does not mean we cannot do it if we choose. If you don't believe me, go and see the Tower — it's never too late.

-13-
A Tale of Two Pubs

The White Horse Inn and the Turf Tavern

The Inns of Oxford make many claims. The oldest and the smallest vie for fame with the watering holes of literary stars, real and imagined. C.S. Lewis, J.R.R. Tolkien and Inspector Endeavour Morse all had their haunts. But the two that I took most to heart are close by one another and are favourites of students and tourists alike.

The Turf Tavern is situated...well, I really know not where in Oxford. For a while, after I had first been taken to The Turf, I was completely unable to relocate it without assistance. It seemed, like Harry Potter's Room of Requirement, to appear from nowhere when it was needed. Approached only through convoluted and narrow passageways, one seemed to go through a little vortex of time and space, to leave the Oxford of today behind and emerge in a lost world of yesterday. The Turf claims to offer 'An education in intoxication' that dates back to 1381, and that's a lot of education.

It is a place you have to stoop to enter, unless of course you are not human and I'm not entirely sure everyone drinking in the tavern was. There is an other-worldliness to it all and the Turf does everything it can, I suspect, to keep up this appearance. To this end perhaps, the Turf boasts a ghost. Rosie is said to haunt the glass wash area where she can be seen to this day washing tankards and awaiting the return of her husband from the English Civil War. Interestingly, during that 17th century war, the Turf was already almost 300 years old.

In the small garden outside, there are tributes to the famous and infamous who have supped there. Bill Clinton was a Rhodes Scholar in Oxford and the Turf claims to be where he did not inhale. And the picture of Gandhi apologises that while the Mahatma himself was not a regular, Ben Kingsley, who won his Oscar for portraying him on screen, was. Margaret Thatcher and Elizabeth Taylor were both regulars but not necessarily, I suspect, at the same parties. And Oscar Wilde, Thomas Hardy and Stephen Hawkins were known to prop up the bar in days gone by.

Leaving the Turf, if you manage to navigate the labyrinth and get yourself back on to Broad Street, you can crawl your way to my second pub. Sandwiched between two parts of the famous and expansive Blackwell's bookshop, the White Horse Inn has been here a long time, but not quite as long as the Turf.

Step down a few steps from the street and you will find yourself in a long and dark and narrow room that clearly has not changed much in a few hundred years. My barman is, surprisingly, a fellow Scot and doesn't flinch at the Scottish banknotes I proffer. Every surface behind the bar is papered with notes and coins from around the world, bearing testament to the cosmopolitan clientele.

Donated Oxford Sports teams' photographs adorn the walls jostling for space with celebrities snapped in the pub.

As much a restaurant now as a pub, the White Horse is especially famous for its pies and it should be for they are fine. Steaming plates of pies and gravy are passed around beneath old beams and placed on the scrubbed pine tables in the window bay, where sitting below street level you can watch the legs of passersby.

Like the Turf Tavern, a sign on the wall reminds visitors that they are in a pub frequented by the famous. Winston Churchill and Bill Clinton are singled out for mention, but in truth it's hard to find a pub in Oxford that doesn't claim Bill as a patron.

'Mind your head,' it says on the door lintel as you leave, and they mean it.

The English pub is something every tourist wants to experience and the two I have chosen to mention, out of the many in Oxford, will never disappoint. Ancient taverns wear their pedigree with pride. Scuffed panelling and uneven floors are reminders that we were here before you were born, before your great great grand parents were born or even thought of, and we will still be here long after your bones have returned to dust.

From our doorway you could have heard the bombers overhead, the cheers of victory with armistice, the celebration of coronation and the screams of martyrs at the fiery stake. You could have found solace from the plague and the fire and the war. And all this time a cavalcade of life has flowed throw our doors, supped our ales and eaten our pies. And for a brief moment, for a small price, you can join that procession, and be part of that parade.

You buy more than beer when you buy a pint in one of these pubs.

-14-
Screen Tests

Eric Gill Doors in the Radcliffe Science Library

Ask nicely, or take along a student with a library card, and you might be able to get into the Radcliffe Science Library on Parks Road. This is very much a working part of the University and tourists are not encouraged, but this building, as well as housing a remarkable collection of scientific tomes, is also the home of a rather special work of 20th century art.

On the first floor, you will find two screens forming the original sliding doors to the Rare Book Room. These screens, composed of six panels carved in low relief of scientists with a strong Oxford connection, were designed and carved by Eric Gill and his assistant Donald Potter in 1935.

Carved front and back from a single piece of wood, each of the oak panels is pierced with the original intention that they should be looked through, like a grill, to the Rare Books Room beyond. However, time marched on and those rare books were moved to a safer location and the room beyond the grill became the office of the Chief Librarian who also goes by the illustrious title of *Keeper of Scientific Books*.

Five of the six panels portray almost household names when it comes to science. At the top, we are shown Roger Bacon, the Franciscan Friar who was a student and then a master at the University and an early European advocate of the scientific method. We also have William Harvey who is shown holding a human heart to remind us that he discovered and documented the circulation of blood. On the left hand door we also have the two Oxford Roberts — Hooke and Boyle — with their microscope and laboratory glassware respectively. And on the right, we have Sir Christopher Wren with the mighty dome of St. Paul's Cathedral in the background and his telescope in front. Remember, he was the Professor of Astronomy in Oxford before he was an architect. But, who is the sixth Oxford scientist in the bottom panel? All the portraits are highly stylised and are identified only by the initials of their subject. The last is 'JJD'. I pondered over this one, but the carving of the wigged man in 18th century garb, with his sunflower did not help. After surrendering to the typed up key, on the wall to the right of the screens, I discovered this to be Johann Jakob Dillenius. I was, I regret to say, none the wiser.

It turns out that the man with the sunflower was an 18th century German botanist who was appointed as the first Sherardian Professor of Botany at the University of Oxford. He was highly regarded by the likes of Linnaeus, who even named a genus of tropical tree after him. But, it's hardly the dome of a cathedral or a law of physics is it? It does rather smack of desperation, I thought, that after the usual scientific suspects had been rounded up and immortalised in oak, one that few have heard of was included, just to make up the numbers.

Thinking this, I suddenly felt sorry for Dillenius having to share the screens with five legends, and having to endure the ignominy that must sting every time someone who admires these panels gets to his portrait and mutters, 'who?'

Who else could have been chosen? In 1935, Dorothy Hodgkin had still to win her Nobel Prize in Chemistry—indeed she had just arrived in Oxford the year before to take up a post-doctoral research fellowship. Florey and Chain were five years away from purifying penicillin, Erwin Schrödinger, the physicist with a fondness for cats, had arrived the year or two before the doors were carved but was only briefly a Fellow of Magdalen, while Tim Berners-Lee, who would give us the world wide web, and Stephen Hawking, his thoughts on the History of Time, were still to be born.

But what of the likes of Edmund Halley, the 18th century Astronomer Royal of comet fame or even Jethro Tull, the pioneering agriculturalist and inventor? Both had strong Oxford connections and might have stood the test of time a little more robustly than Dillenius.

However, the reason I had blagged my way into the library was not because of the subjects of the screen, but because of its creator. The artist Eric Gill is now known mostly through his font design — look on any word-processing package and you will likely find his eponymous typeface, *Gill Sans*, as an option. And, you will find *Perpetua*, which he also designed. As well as being a typographer, he was a graphic artist, sculptor and printmaker, designing such diverse commissions as the statuary outside the old BBC building in London and the definitive stamps of King George VI. He has countless war memorials and signage to his name in Oxford, London and beyond.

His religious fervour was perhaps the reason he was involved in so many ecclesiastical projects, and his sexual proclivities the explanation for his abundant erotica. His personal sex life was exuberant as well as incestuous and he scandalised even the bohemian society in which he lived. Indeed, his sexuality has for many overshadowed and sullied his body of work. If you like his work, as I do, it becomes necessary to separate the artistry before you and the man who created it. You do not need to admire, or even like, the latter to love the former.

And it is this notion of separation, which is important here. Although the screen commemorates six (or at least five) legendary scientists, it is really their work that is being celebrated, not the men themselves. Just as Gill's work should not be viewed through a filter of moral judgement about his personal life, we should be able to marvel at Wren's architecture free from any concern about his freemasonry, or feel a pulse without having to think about Harvey's obsessive bird-watching.

We live in a society much affected by the cult of celebrity — a cult that relies on the personification of achievement. This is bad enough, but becomes particularly inane when the 'achievement' in question is simply being famous itself. Think of the pseudo-celebrities and game show contestants who fill the pages of pulp magazines. It is important to separate the work from the person, and to judge the work in distinction from the worker. If we do this it may quickly become apparent that there is no work to celebrate.

Here, Gill focussed on the people and portrayed them with an example of their greatest work. Perhaps he could have let the work stand for itself, but he chose not to. There is celebrity in science, just as in any other sphere of human endeavour, and although we should be more interested in the idea than the thinker, the provenance of the thought may influence how much credence we give it. After all, if I had not known that Eric Gill had designed these screens would I have made the effort to see them?

-15-
Tea at 4 o'clock

The College Senior Common Room

'Tea at four in the SCR?' 'Of course, that would be delightful.' Whether we like it or not, we can hardly say that we live in a classless society. Even our American cousins, who often ridicule the British class system, live in a society frankly riven with elitism. Admittedly, our Prime Minister and many of his cabinet are former public school boys (Cameron himself, an old Etonian), while President Obama is just a backwater boy who rose to the highest office in the land, or so we are led to believe. However, on both sides of the Atlantic we spend a lot of time and effort building the necessary barriers to keep some people in, and others out.

Divisions are certainly alive and well and living in Oxford, and are especially notable in the academic arrangements for leisure. The common rooms frequented by undergraduates, postgraduates and staff are respectively known as Junior, Middle and Senior Common Rooms and each group firmly knows its place. My son, a postgraduate student, showed me proudly round his MCR — a comfortable, if dishevelled, collection of sofas in a large, what looked like 17th century, room adorned by restoration portraits, a piano and tea making facilities. The JCR is little different from the sixth form common room at school and takes the rough and tumble of its youthful clientele on the chin. The SCR, on the other hand, is an altogether more stately affair.

Reminiscent of the staff room at a rather well-to-do public school, this area of academic calm bears the fixtures and fittings appropriate to the status of its incumbents. There is sherry in a cut crystal decanter on the mahogany side table. A bronze bust of a former master sits comfortably in the deep window sill, while a long case clock with a tick, and a perceptibly distinct tock, measures out the hours until the end of Trinity term. A large central table is filled with the day's papers and a magazine rack carries the latest editions from the worlds of business, science and arts. Rich rugs and good curtains soften the scene while the room is filled with light from large windows overlooking the quad. There is cake for tea at four o'clock and an oil painting of Venice on the wall — and it probably is a Canaletto.

Quite how I ended up sitting — or lounging — sipping tea from a crested cup, is neither here nor there, but it felt right, even though, for the sake of propriety, I would like to have reported that it didn't. This was how an afternoon break should be, and as far as Oxford dons are concerned, how it has been for as long as anyone can remember. I don't know what every SCR in Oxford looks like, but I suspect the one I sampled was a fair representation of them all. This was the members' enclosure, the back room, the inner sanctum. Indeed, this was what the BA Executive Lounge would look like if British Airways had been around for 800 years.

But, it's not really class that divides in Oxford, but seniority and that is quite a different thing. Postgraduates, with their extra three of four years under their belts, can hardly bear to be in the same room as undergrads. All that silliness of youth, which only a few summers before was shared, is now a source of extreme irritation. Fast forward a decade, or in some cases three or four decades, and you can understand why staff need their own distinct space. And a room for the grown-ups might as well be beautiful as well as functional, for this group is hardly going to trash the place or host a toga party.

It might be easy to feel discomfort in such a setting if overawed by it, but perhaps I am just too old to think that I don't deserve it. I enjoyed every privileged moment in that bright, beautiful room, perhaps because my own experience in academia had been so different.

As you rise up through the university system in Oxford the privileges multiply and why shouldn't they? Not so elsewhere in my experience. There, the professors — and I was one of them — get the chipped cups in the staff room like everyone else. But in Oxford, tenure brings sherry and the Financial Times...and tea at four o'clock.

-16-
Like Looking for an Apostrophe in a Bookshop

Blackwell's on Broad Street

If you are a book lover, as you step over the threshold of Blackwell's in Oxford, you might be forgiven for wondering if you have suddenly been fatally struck by a falling piece of masonry or perhaps been the victim of a random act of drive-by shooting. You will not have felt the blow nor heard the shot, but you will have slipped from this world to the next. For what happens as you step inside the shop must be the nearest thing to entering the pearly gates and crossing the threshold of heaven that any bibliophile is likely to experience on Earth.

This is not a bookshop; this is a book paradise. It invites us, in a rather understated way, 'to browse one of the finest bookshops in the world.' Leaving room for doubt is understandably English, but disingenuous nonetheless. The scale, the breadth, the depth and the sheer overpowering heft of Blackwell's places it at the top of the list. As well as what appears to be every book on every subject ever written, you can buy such esoteric delights as *Harry Potter* translated into Ancient Greek and a set of *Scrabble* for playing in Latin.

But, in addition to well-stocked shelves, you are also offered provenance. There are photos, mementos and quotes sprinkled around the walls of the shop. Discretely placed, so as to be stumbled upon rather than tripped over, you will find a photograph of a sitting US president walking outside the shop carrying a Blackwell's bag of books; you will, if you look for it, find the 1993 Royal Warrant issued by the Lord Chamberlain, decreeing that Blackwell's is the Queen's bookseller; close by you will find one of the original bookshelves from the much smaller 1879 shop as well as paintings of dons and students poring over new books, and autographed photos of grateful authors thanking the shop staff for their care and attention during signings. The shop even figures in the books that it sells and quotations from several novels including Evelyn Waugh's *Brideshead Revisited* adorn the walls.

And just when you thought you might be in a really good, book shop, but a book shop nevertheless, you descend the stairs and find yourself in the underground vault that is the Norrington Room. This, like the treasure chamber of an Egyptian king undisturbed by grave robbers, reveals itself to be full — on around 5 kilometres of shelving there are more than 160,000 books for this is the largest single book room in Europe. But where exactly are you? Without realising it you have slipped beneath the quad of Trinity College and indeed the room was named after Sir Arthur Norrington, the publisher and President of Trinity College when the room was opened after it was excavated in 1966.

Lest I appear to be overly effusive about this corner of Oxford, let me highlight one thing — the strange case of the missing apostrophe. Most bookshelves will have a corner devoted to poetry; Westminster Abbey has a Poets' Corner where the mortal remains of several of our greatest writers are interred, such as Chaucer, Tennyson, Dickens and Hardy. Blackwell's has a cosy nook on the first floor where all its poetry books are shelved around an old marble fireplace in a small hexagonal room. The sign above the entrance reads, 'Poet s Corner.' Now, I checked the other side of the hanging sign in case this was merely a typo, but on the reverse was the same un-apostrophised declaration. I looked around the shelves and all the other apostrophes were present and correct. 'Milton's Selected Poetry and Prose' was there, as were numerous editions of 'Everyman's Poetry.' I even checked around the shelves of the adjacent department of Language and Literature and there was no sign of the missing punctuation mark. I flicked through a few books and, with the exception of course of William Faulkner, all seemed to have the requisite number of apostrophes. Quite where the punctuation had gone was a mystery.

The fact that there is a space might suggest that one was intended, but you can never be sure, even though Blackwell's has been careful with its own apostrophe. Unlike Harrods and Boots and Selfridges, who have over the years dispensed with such titular punctuation, Blackwell's still has its.

Despite my fully paid up membership of the apostrophe police, I decided I would turn a blind eye on this occasion. What might be a grammatical lapse, may in fact be a deliberate spiritual attempt to introduce an imperfection into an otherwise perfect order, in deference to the unique perfection of God. Or it may even be nothing more that an elaborate ruse to make people like me write about the shop. But, that would never work, would it?

-17-
Croquet in the Rain

The Obsession of Sports

Watching a sport that you have never seen played before, and of which you know none of the rules, is quite a thought-provoking experience. You look for patterns of behaviours and try to formulate the rules for yourself; you try to build up a picture of the whole from small examples and observations. In other words, you exercise your inductive powers of reasoning.

Despite what Sherlock Holmes said, he 'deduced' nothing, but rather he 'induced'. Deduction is a reduction starting with the big picture, the universal law, the rules and works downwards to a specific situation. Induction, on the other hand is all about an increase from component pieces of evidence that collectively allow you to arrive at those rules or the law in question, or in Holmes' case, the identity of the criminal. Induction is what we do in science when we make an observation, then another and then another and from these findings formulate an hypothesis, which if supported by further evidence might become a theory or even a law to explain the generality of things.

With a new and unfamiliar situation, where there is no rule-book, or at least not one that anyone has thought to share with you, all that is left is the power of induction to work it all out.

While watching a croquet match on Balliol's sports field, I ended up trying to induce so hard I almost didn't notice the rain. Now, although this was my first croquet match, I had rather expected sunshine, and parasols and wicker hampers of strawberries and the like. Instead, I received rain of the unremitting sort and two deadly earnest teams of players who were competing here in Oxford in what is the largest croquet tournament in the world. (That latter claim, however, has all the force of America's Baseball World Series — I mean, what other countries are even in the tournament?) No, this was not a gentle, Edwardian pastime for the lace-trimmed ladies, this was Sport and it looked serious.

Croquet is clearly quite a thing in Oxford. Charles Dodgeson, the Christ Church Maths lecturer who is better known as Lewis Carroll, put a lot of croquet into *Alice's Adventures in Wonderland*. But, in his version of the game the mallets were live flamingos, the balls live hedgehogs and the hoops were improvised by playing card cum soldiers. What I was watching was only slightly less odd.

At first it seems that you hit one ball against another with the intent of driving the struck ball through a wire hoop, or wicket, as I was informed. Rather like snooker on grass, I thought, with hoops (sorry, wickets) instead of pockets. But, quickly that notion gets dispelled as all sorts of strange things seem to happen. There does seem to be an importance in the positioning of balls at the end of a shot—again reminiscent of snooker — but the depth of strategy, evident in the furrowed brows of the players contemplating each and every shot, was much more akin to chess on grass. What on Earth was going on here?

I have to confess the rain got the better of me and I retired to the comfort of my College room — and the apparently Byzantine rules of croquet remained thoroughly un-induced.

Sometimes you have to admit defeat, especially when you're wet.   To have stayed I would have needed a stronger dose of obsession that I possess. Sport is taken seriously in Oxford — all sports. And by sports, I mean all the usual pursuits like Rowing, and Rugby and Athletics as well as the more esoteric ones like Caving, Ultimate Frisbee and even Cheerleading.   But, look through the list of the Oxford University Sports Clubs and a few you've never heard of pop out. What, for instance, are Octopush, Korfball and Krav-Tardemet? Turns out they are a mix of netball and basketball, underwater hockey and a modern martial art specifically created for self-defence — but not necessarily in that order.

I was never a great sports fan, perhaps because I was never very adept at any sport. I realise now that at school I was only offered the very basic options of soccer, rugby or cross-country running—in none of which I excelled or even passed muster. Perhaps, if I had been offered the option of Korfball or that Krav thingy I might have found my niche. Perhaps, I was an Olympian hiding his talent under his note to get out of P.E. Or perhaps not.

I just never thought sport was important enough to get worked up about or put any effort into. And I certainly did not have the determination I had just witnessed on the soggy croquet lawn or that you will see watching the rowing eights on the river or the men's varsity lacrosse. But sport, I have realised, is important — it matters because it doesn't matter at all. Life is complicated and turbulent with many ups and downs and roundabouts that can disorientate as well as dishearten. Many things matter because they affect our work, our finances, our loves and our health. Sport allows us to escape and to care about something, the outcome of which makes no difference to us in the long run. As such, it is therapy simultaneously for body and mind.

Perhaps, I should give croquet in the rain another go. Maybe if they used flamingos.

-18-
Picking Up the Pieces

The Becket Window, Christ Church Cathedral

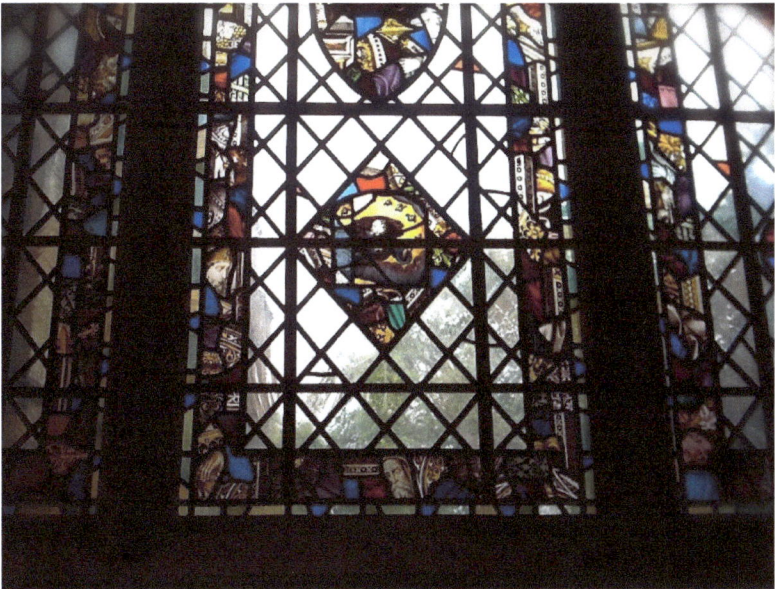

Look up and look closely.

The ribbons of multicoloured glass that frame the panels of the lower lights in the window reveal themselves not to be deliberate images, but collages of broken fragments — shards of glass collected from the ruins of bombed out churches in London during the Second World War. This is medieval artistry destroyed by war and given new life in the majestic setting of the Cathedral of

Christ Church, Oxford. Most visit this college and come to its church to marvel at the famous fan-vaulted ceiling and many miss the Becket window tucked away in the side chapel, but this in many ways is the church's greatest and rarest treasure.

The top panels of the tracery are as bright and vivid today as when they were installed in around 1320 — making it the oldest stained glass in the place. In a central panel, there is a kneeling figure in ecclesiastical garb. Behind him there are soldiers with ominously raised swords, for these are his assassins. The victim is the 12th century Archbishop of Canterbury Thomas Becket and this is one of the very few surviving images of the martyred saint. The lower half of the window is thought originally to have contained a larger image of Becket, but this portion was destroyed on the orders of that Church lover Henry VIII. What we can see today is a reconstruction, reuse and recycling of what would have otherwise been lost.

The small 14th century image of Becket is thought to have survived because his features were not apparent in the clear glass fragment that was his head. Today this has been replaced by a plain pink piece of stained glass, still featureless — perhaps to protect him from any further royal rout.

This is a window that makes you pause, or at least it should. In the cathedral you are drowned in the grandeur of centuries of art and worship; you walk on the graves of dignitaries, and the walls are lined with commemoration. In short, there is a lot to see and altogether too much to take in, but you should take the moment or two necessary to stand before the Becket window and think about what it represents.

No matter what bombs are thrown, and what beauty they destroy, we have the capacity, quite literally, to pick up the pieces and rebuild. In this case, there could be no attempt to recreate what was there before — too much of the original windows from which these fragments fell was irretrievably lost — but what has been done is simultaneously a silent homage to medieval craftsmen and a nose thumbing at iconoclastic zeal.

By taking pieces of robes, slices of trees and quarters of faces, and welding them together, a modern yet medieval beauty has emerged. Henry VIII did not succeed, nor did Nazi bombs. And a window that was originally designed to celebrate a slain archbishop has become not only symbolic of that saint, but also of renaissance in general.

There are undoubtedly mixed emotions to be felt before this work of art, or should I say works of art. On the one hand, we are witnessing a mob hit on the altar of a church, as well as the tangible brutality towards art and beauty that all wars bring. But, on the other, we are also presented with the resolution of belief and the tremendous human capacity for healing and reconciliation. We have before us what can be achieved by putting aside the past, moving on from the pain and concentrating on rediscovering the beauty that is always there, if we look.

It was Goethe who said, 'Thinking is more interesting than knowing, but less interesting than looking'. Standing in front of this window, I spent a while looking and since then I have spent much longer thinking. Like most, I have scarcely arrived at the point of knowing, although I am hopeful. But it began with looking — it almost always does — and the visual stimulus lights the spark of thought, of new ideas, of new wonder. Observation is at the heart of science, but it is also undoubtedly the genesis of all creative thought. Whether we observe the world around us or the inner world of our consciousness, what we see lights the way and helps us choose a path to follow.

Along the way, we collect the fragments, sort them through, piece them together and find the new patchwork that is formed. You may discover a synthesis of new ideas. Or you may even find you have created ribbons of medieval coloured glass to delight a new generation and pay respect to one long gone.

The Becket window is a metaphor, but it is also a work of art fused across the centuries, showing what can be done when we choose to begin by looking.

-19-
Through the Wardrobe Door

Looking for Narnia just off the High Street

Tour guides delight in pointing it out. They love to enchant their customers with the tale, even if it is only half-true.

The story goes that a lifetime ago, a Fellow of nearby Magdalen College would regularly walk down this lane, past the old lamp post and catch sight of the carved lion's head on the door, framed by two fauns. The same Fellow would later write one of the best loved children's books of the 20th century that would prominently figure a lamp post, a faun called Mr Tumnus and a majestic lion called Aslan. The Oxford don in question was C.S.

Lewis and the book was *The Lion, the Witch and the Wardrobe*, published in 1950.

If you stand close to the door today, or on any day, you can watch a succession of tourists all nosing their way along the lane before finally finding the door they have been looking for. Pictures will be taken, Aslan's wooden mane might be stroked and then they will hurry along to see the next thing on their list — the Rad Cam or the Bodleian Library or perhaps they may file out on to High Street to find refreshment. Occasionally, one or two visitors will linger, spending longer than the requisite tourist moment. They will ponder in silence the door, wonder what lies behind it and imagine a frozen land that they once heard about in a story.

To come face to face with inspiration, to stand in the footsteps of a great creative force, encourages one to imagine what he or she must have thought. Of course, it wasn't necessarily that lamp post, or that carved lion's head, or even that faun that sparked Lewis's magical tale. There are other contenders. There is a lone lamp post in the driveway of a private school in Belfast, where Lewis grew up, and there is a brass door knob on his local church rectory's door there with — you guessed it — a lion's head with a flowing mane.

Whatever the source, Lewis conjured his tale of magic and morality that has enchanted children for the last six decades while he was in Oxford. This is a place in which it is easy to be creative. All around there is beauty and inspiration. The very walls of the buildings are hung with splendour as well as constant reminders that great people walked these streets and great ideas were crafted here. Even as a visitor, it does not take too long to be lost in thought; for those who live and work here it must be an occupational hazard.

Lewis spent almost thirty years in Oxford as a Fellow and Tutor in English Literature before moving to 'the other place', as they refer to Cambridge here, to take up a Chair in Medieval and Renaissance Literature. His academic career was distinguished but his passion and creativity was unconstrained by the quads and his popular works would find an enormous following. He would write many books, including another six about the magical land of Narnia, before he died a week short of his 65th birthday on 22 November 1963 — the same day JFK was assassinated.

Today, however, the Aslan door leads not into Narnia but into Brasenose College. Search the college's website today for information on the door and you will find none. Type in Aslan, Narnia, even C.S. Lewis, and you get no hits. Others would be boasting about such a connection, but this is Oxford and a mid-20th century story for children, no matter how popular, does not figure highly in a college's sense of its own history. It's not arrogance; it's a different perspective. These colleges were here 500 years before Narnia and plan to be around long after such a storybook land is forgotten. There is a long-term game plan at work in Oxford that has little time for the here and now. There is continuity in the stones of these colleges: unbroken lines of scholarship that span the centuries. And, they do not give in easily to fashions and fads. Lewis and his lion are doubtless seen as nothing more than a temporary fascination of Oxford's tourists.

If he is still around in another hundred years or so, and if the tourists are still searching along the walls of the lane for a carved lion's head in the 22nd or 23rd centuries, then Brasenose may concede that Lewis deserves a mention. Longevity is a hallmark of classicism and it is the only badge of honour that this place seems to recognise. And that's one of the magical things about Oxford. Flash-in-the-pan celebrity is assiduously ignored here with all the disdain the University can muster. But stick around, and after a few centuries it might even notice you're here.

-20-
'And not make dreams your master'

A Day of Endings and Beginnings in the Sheldonian

Some live in the here and now; others in the past. Yet others, perhaps the most hopeful amongst us, live wishfully in the future. Their lives are built on a scaffolding of hope, while others dwell on the regrets of what might have been. It is easy for such thoughts to take over and master our lives. But, neither the past nor the future can offer what the very moment we are now living in can. The present affords us a connection to the world that is as real as it will get.

All experience is, however, a form of fantasy. We engage with the world through imperfect senses and the model of the present that we reconstruct in our cerebral cortex is what we call reality. If that model is based on real time inputs — the sights and sounds around us at a particular moment, the scents of the present as well as the thoughts they evoke — then it has a better chance of reflecting that reality.

That is the basis of what has come to be known as mindfulness, and I am a subscriber to the notion that this approach to managing our thoughts is one of our best chances for mental health and perspective. But not today.

The morning is overcast with a chance of rain and I am sitting on a train heading for a city where I know there will be sunshine. A city made of honey-coloured stone, with spires and lawns, but I am aware that it may be my last trip to Oxford, for today I am going to a graduation.

The last years have slipped down easily like a fine wine but all at once the glass is almost drained. I can savour the taste that memories leave and reflect on my time on that bench in Broad Street outside Balliol where I spent so many hours. From there, I watched Oxford walk by in the form of its students and shopkeepers and tourists, and I watched the yellow Oxford stones looking back at me — silent, unmoved and ever so uncaring that I was watching them. Oxford was there before I came and it was quietly confident that it would be there long after I had gone. When that time came, the city would reclaim its bench and with it the chance to beguile its next visitor.

What would the future hold? Would I return? Could I, without my connection, now that my son had graduated, had left the city for his new job in London? For the mindful, to ponder the 'what might be' is a largely fruitless exercise, but not as much as living in the past, swaddled in warm memories to keep out the cold of the here and now.

Oxford *is* that city of dreaming spires we have all heard about. It does enchant and intoxicate in equal measure, but it is strangely not of the here and now. It seems, at least today, all about the past and all about the future. The present, the moment filled with a heart-beat and a breath, seems to be somewhere else.

Today is a swirl of pride and sadness. Something is undoubtedly over, and something new is clearly beginning. However, what is not so clear to me is what is happening right now, this moment, as my son stands and walks across the floor of the Sheldonian Theatre — gowned in scarlet and blue to take possession of his doctorate. I shift in what have to be the most uncomfortable seats in Oxford and strain to see the moment that he has been working towards for almost four years. All I can see in this majestic amphitheatre built by Sir Christopher Wren is the view from my bench, the strolls through galleries and museums, the cafes and book shops, the libraries and colleges, the river with its punts and ducks. All I can see between the gilding and the paintings in this grand hall are my memories and my hopes. Before the moment is over, if indeed it ever takes place at all, I am lost between the past and the future, but I am certainly not in the present.

As my 'now' slips through my fingers and becomes my past, perhaps I can make sense of it as well as think about what's next. Today my mindfulness has failed me utterly. I am devoid of the moment and am wandering through the past I have so enjoyed. And I am dreaming. But, I tell no one of my dreams, lest said out loud they blow away, or worse, hold me to a course. My moment of 'now' has become a reflection on 'then' and I am fine with that. Yes, we must hold to the present, but on a day like today, amongst these stones, I can dream, can I not? As long as those dreams can be recognised for what they are, and they do not become my master.

About the Author

Allan Gaw, MD, PhD, FRCPath, FFPM, PGCert Med Ed is a Scottish writer and educator. He has been a clinical academic for over 25 years. Most recently he was Professor & Director of the Clinical Research Facility at Queen's University Belfast, and he previously worked at the University of Glasgow and UT Southwestern in Dallas, Texas, none of which were built of honey-coloured stone.

He is passionate about the need to develop those key writing and presentation skills that are essential in professional life. In addition to over twenty books, he regularly publishes articles on a range of subjects and a blog entitled *The Business of Discovery* (researchet.wordpress.com)

If you would like to learn more about him and his work, visit his website www.allangaw.com or follow him on twitter @ResearchET.

Other Works by the Author

Gaw A. WriteEasy: A Strategy for More Effective Scientific Writing. SA Press, Glasgow, 2014.

Gaw A. WordEasy: The Commonest Grammatical Mistakes in Formal Writing & How to Avoid Them. SA Press, Glasgow, 2013.

Gaw A. SpeakEasy: 7 Ingredients for Effective Presentations. SA Press, Glasgow, 2012.

Gaw A. Our Speaker Today – A Guide to Effective Lecturing. SA Press, Glasgow, 2010.

Gaw A. Abstract Expressions – A Quick Guide to Writing Effective Abstracts for Conferences and Papers. SA Press, Glasgow, 2011.

Gaw A. Born in Scandal: Frances Oldham Kelsey and the development of pharmaceutical regulation. SA Press, Glasgow, 2013.

Gaw A & Burns MHJ. On Moral Grounds – Lessons from the History of Research Ethics. SA Press, Glasgow, 2011.

Gaw A. Trial by Fire – Lessons from the History of Clinical Trials. SA Press, Glasgow, 2009.

www.ingramcontent.com/pod-product-compliance
Lightning Source LLC
Chambersburg PA
CBHW040936110426
42739CB00026B/6